CLAYTON

D0741994

OCEANS ALIVE

Octopuses

by Ann Herriges

CONTRA COSTA COUNTY LIBRARY

3 1901 04162 3317

BLASTOFF!
2
READERS

BELLWETHER MEDIA • MINNEAPOLIS, MN

Note to Librarians, Teachers, and Parents:

Blastoff! Readers are carefully developed by literacy experts and combine standards-based content with developmentally appropriate text.

Level 1 provides the most support through repetition of high-frequency words, light text, predictable sentence patterns, and strong visual support.

Level 2 offers early readers a bit more challenge through varied simple sentences, increased text load, and less repetition of high-frequency words.

Level 3 advances early-fluent readers toward fluency through increased text and concept load, less reliance on visuals, longer sentences, and more literary language.

Whichever book is right for your reader, Blastoff! Readers are the perfect books to build confidence and encourage a love of reading that will last a lifetime!

This edition first published in 2007 by Bellwether Media.

No part of this publication may be reproduced in whole or in part without written permission of the publisher. For information regarding permission, write to Bellwether Media Inc., Attention: Permissions Department, Post Office Box 1C, Minnetonka, MN 55345-9998.

Library of Congress Cataloging-in-Publication Data
Herriges, Ann.
  Octopuses / by Ann Herriges.
    p. cm. – (Blastoff! readers) (Oceans alive!)
Summary: "Simple text and supportive images introduce beginning readers to octopuses. Intended for students in kindergarten through third grade."
  Includes bibliographical references and index.
  ISBN-10: 1-60014-019-X (hardcover : alk. paper)
  ISBN-13: 978-1-60014-019-8 (hardcover : alk. paper)
  1. Octopuses—Juvenile literature. I. Title. II. Series. III. Series: Oceans alive!

  QL430.3.O2H47 2006
  594'.56—dc22   2006002771

Text copyright © 2007 by Bellwether Media.
Printed in the United States of America.

Table of Contents

Octopuses have soft bodies.

They can fit their bodies
through small spaces.

eyes

Octopuses have a head.

They have two large eyes.

Octopuses have eight arms.

There are **webs** of skin between the arms.

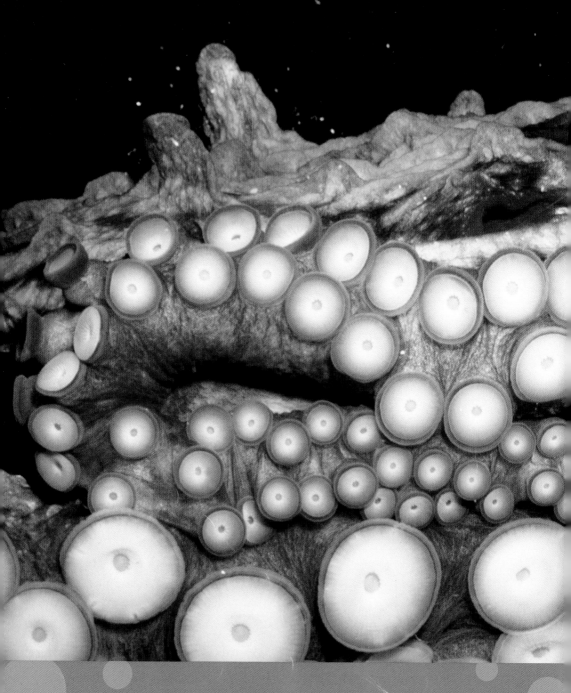

Octopus arms have **suckers**.

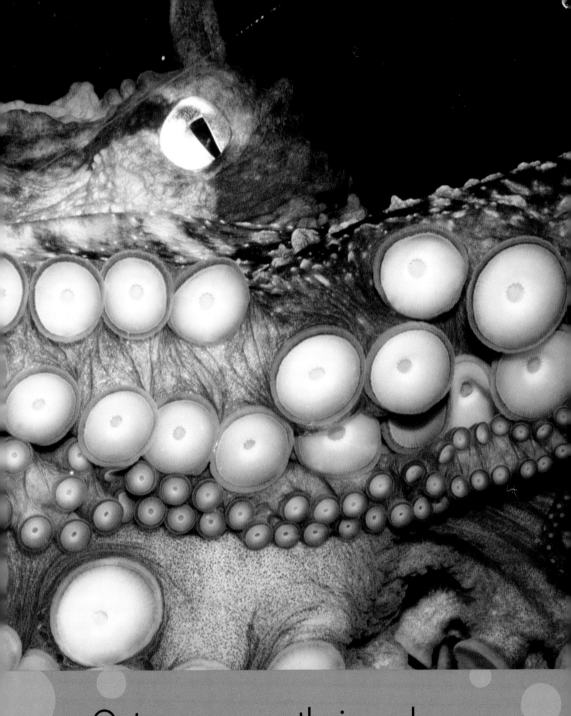

Octopuses use their suckers
to smell and to taste.

Octopuses also use the
suckers to grab things and
to hold onto rocks.

They use their suckers to crawl on the ocean floor.

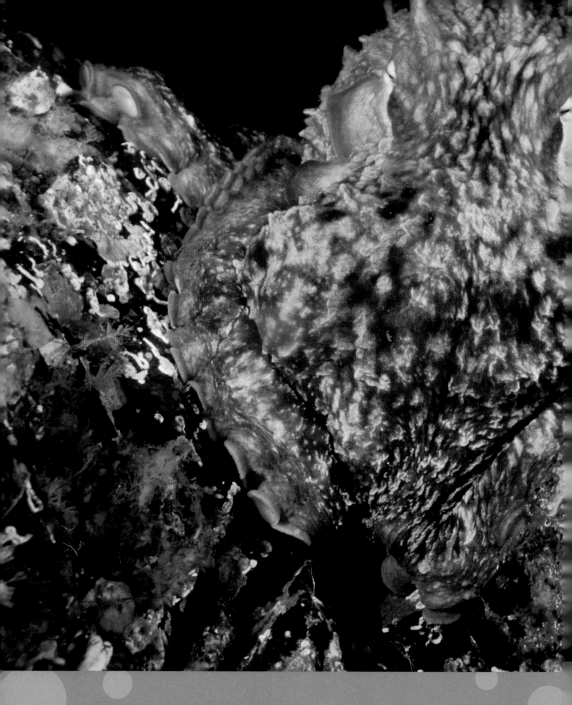

Octopuses live alone in rocky **dens**.

den

They leave their dens to hunt for crabs, clams, and lobsters.

Octopuses poke their arms
between rocks to search for
their **prey**.

They bring the prey back to
their dens to eat.

Octopuses hide
from **predators**.

They can change color to
match their **surroundings**.

An octopus can squirt dark **ink** into the water. This surprises a predator.

Swoosh! The octopus escapes. It changes color and swims away.

Glossary

den—an animal's home; octopuses make their dens between rocks or inside coral caves; sometimes they build their own dens.

ink—a dark liquid that octopuses can squirt from their bodies

predator—an animal that hunts other animals for food; seals, whales, and eels are some of the predators that eat octopuses.

prey—an animal that is hunted by another animal for food; octopuses eat crabs, clams, snails, and lobsters; some octopuses eat other octopuses.

suckers—round cup-shaped parts on an octopus's arms; suckers can bend and stretch to hold onto things.

surroundings—the area around something; the octopus can change its color to match the plants, rocks, and coral around it.

web—the fold of skin between the arms of an octopus

To Learn More

AT THE LIBRARY

Andreae, Giles. *Commotion in the Ocean.* Wilton, Conn.: Tiger Tales, 2002.

Langeland, Deirdre. *Octopus' Den.* Norwalk, Conn.: Soundprints, 1997.

Most, Bernard. *My Very Own Octopus.* New York: Harcourt Brace Jovanovich, 1980.

Pitcher, Caroline. *Nico's Octopus.* New York: Crocodile Books, 2003.

Roop, Connie. *Octopus Under the Sea.* New York: Scholastic, 2001.

Tate, Suzanne. *Oozey Octopus: A Tale of a Clever Critter.* Nags Head, N.C.: Nags Head Art, 2000.

Wallace, Karen. *Gentle Giant Octopus.* Cambridge, Mass.: Candlewick Press, 1998.

ON THE WEB
Learning more about octopuses is as easy as 1, 2, 3.

1. Go to www.factsurfer.com

2. Enter "octopuses" into search box.

3. Click the "Surf" button and you will see a list of related web sites.

With factsurfer.com, finding more information is just a click away.

Index

The photographs in this book are reproduced through the courtesy of: Stuart Westmorland/Getty Images, front cover; Steven Hunt/Getty Images, pp. 4-5; Aqua Image/Alamy, pp. 6-7; David Fleetham/Getty Images, pp. 8-9, 14-15; Ken Lucas/Getty Images, pp. 10-11; Lionel Isy-Schwart/Getty Images, pp. 12-13; Brandon Cole Marine Photography/Alamy, pp. 16-17; Reinhard Dirscherl/Alamy, pp. 18-19; Jeff Rotman/Alamy, pp. 20-21.